PRAYERS FOR YOUNG PEOPLE

Professor Barclay is a distinguished scholar,
an exceptionally gifted preacher and a reg-
ular broadcaster. His writings for the *British
Weekly* were very popular and for 20 years
from 1950 a full page every week was given
to them. From 1963 until 1974 he was Professor of Divinity and Biblical Criticism at
Glasgow University. He was a Member of
the Advisory Committee working on the
New English Bible and also a Member of the
Apocrypha Panel of Translators. In 1975 he
was appointed a Visiting Professor at the
University of Strathclyde for a period of
three years where he will lecture on Ethics,
and in the same year – jointly with the Rev.
Professor James Stewart – he received the
1975 Citation from the American theological
organization The Upper Room; the first
time it has been awarded outside America.
His extremely popular Bible Study Notes
using his own translation of the New Testa-
ment have achieved a world-wide sale.

WILLIAM BARCLAY

Prayers for Young People

Collins

FOUNT PAPERBACKS

First published by Wm. Collins Sons & Co. Ltd. 1963
First issued in Fontana Books 1966
Fourteenth Impression June 1976

Reprinted in Fount Paperbacks March 1977

© William Barclay 1963
Made and printed in Great Britain by
William Collins Sons & Co Ltd

For Fiona

You and Your Prayers

Prayer is like any other great and valuable gift or possession—we will never get the best and the most from it, unless we learn to use it aright. This means that there are certain things which we must always bear in mind when we pray.

i. The very first thing that we must remember is that God wants us to pray to him. There are times when people make it quite clear that we are a nuisance to them, and when quite clearly they cannot be bothered with us. No one is ever a nuisance to God. Once when Jesus talked to God, he used a word to address God which to us is a foreign word. He called God, 'Abba, Father' (Mark 14:36). Afterwards Paul said that this word Abba is the word that any Christian can use when he talks to God (Romans 8:15). It is just not possible to translate this word Abba into English. It was the word which a young child used in Palestine in the time of Jesus when he talked to his father, just as to this day Arab boys and girls call their father *jaba*. It is really the eastern word for Daddy. This means that we can talk to God just as easily and just as simply as we talk to our own father in our own home.

Once someone asked a wise man how to set about praying. The wise man said: 'Just take a chair and put it opposite you, and think to yourself that God is sitting on that chair, and just talk to him in the way that you would talk to your closest friend.'

Prayer should not be unnatural and difficult; it should

be as natural and as easy as talking to the person you know and love best of all.

In prayer we do not need any special words or any special language. We do not need to say 'thou' and 'thee'. That is the way the Bible has it, because that is the way in which people used ordinarily to talk long ago. We can use to God the same kind of language as we use every day. We do not need to be in any special place to pray. We can pray anywhere. Of course, it is easier to pray in some places than it is in others. In a church or in a great cathedral we cannot help having a feeling of reverence. But God is just as near us in a room in our own home, on the street, in a class-room, on a playing-field, on a hill-top, as he is in any church or in any cathedral. We do not need to be in any special position to pray to God. We can pray walking along the road, sitting in a chair, standing on a moor or by the sea-shore, even lying in bed, just as well as we can pray kneeling. When we pray, all we have got to do is just to speak to God as we speak to our best friend.

ii. When we pray we have to remember that we do not need to squeeze things out of God, as if he had to be persuaded into giving them to us. God wants to give us his good gifts even more than we want to ask him for them. Sometimes when we want something from a human person, we have to pester him into giving it to us; we have to break down his resistance. But God is not like that. He is more eager to give than we are to ask.

iii. Of course, that does not mean that, if we want something, we have only to ask for it. It is very important to remember that God knows what is good for us far better than we know ourselves; and there are times when we pray for things which in the end would not be for our good. When we were very young we often wanted to do things like playing with matches; or we often wanted

8

far more sweets or fruit than was good for us; or we wanted to do something which more experienced people knew could only lead to trouble. When that kind of thing happened, those who loved us had to refuse to give us what we wanted. Sometimes God has to do that. It is not that God does not answer our prayers; it is that God answers them, not in our way, but in his.

There is a problem here. If God knows everything, if God knows what is good for us better than we know ourselves, why bother to pray at all? If God knows it all, what need is there for us to speak to him? We talk about God knowing our secret thoughts; if we go to Church at all, we must have heard the prayer which begins: 'Almighty God, unto whom all hearts be open, all desires known, and from whom no secrets are hid'; if this is so, what is the sense in praying to one who knows what we want to pray for before we pray for it?

This is something about which we must think, for we certainly will not ever really pray, if we think in our heart of hearts that prayer is really a waste of time. Let us think about this in relation to the five different kinds of prayer.

There is the prayer which we call *invocation*. Invocation literally means a calling in. In the prayer of invocation we ask for God's presence with us, or, to put it better, because God is always with us, we ask God to make us aware that he is with us. Now, one of the great stories of Jesus after his resurrection tells how he met in with two people who were on the road from Jerusalem to Emmaus. They did not recognize him, but they were thrilled and fascinated by the things which he told them. They came near to the village and to the house where these two people lived. And then it says of Jesus: 'He made as though he would have gone further.' But they begged him to come into their house and visit them, and so he

9

did (Luke 24:28,29). There is about God and Jesus what we can only call a very wonderful courtesy. We cannot go into someone else's house without an invitation. It would be very impolite and very discourteous to burst in all uninvited; we wait until we are asked. God is like that. God wants to come into our life; he wants to meet us; but he waits until we ask him to come in to us. Of course, God shows us in all kinds of ways that he wants us to know him and to love him and to talk to him; but, like a courteous guest, he waits until we invite him in just as Jesus did on the road to Emmaus long ago. That is the first reason why we must speak to him, although he knows it all already.

There is the prayer which we call *confession*. Confession means telling God about the wrong things that we have done, saying that we are sorry for them, and asking him to forgive us for them. We know what happens at home. We do something wrong, and then we regret it. We know quite well that our parents really know that we are sorry, and we know quite well that they will forgive us. But between us and them there is a kind of invisible barrier, there is the feeling that something is wrong, there is a kind of atmosphere of unhappiness and strangeness, until we go to them and say: 'I'm sorry I was bad; I'll try not to do it again.' And immediately we have gone to them and said it, things are all right again. It is just the same with us and God. We know that nothing that we can do will stop God loving us; we know that he is always willing to forgive us; but things are not right between us and him until we go to him and say that we are sorry for what we have done.

There is the prayer which we call *thanksgiving*. Thanksgiving means thanking God for all the good gifts which he has given to us. One of the great dangers of life is that we should take things for granted just because they come to us regularly and every day. And it is never enough just to feel grateful to those who are kind to us; we must sometimes express our gratitude in words. A great many people have had an experience like this. They have known when they were young that their parents were very good and very kind to them, but they never said thank you and never said how grateful they were. Then the day came when their parents died, and when they looked back, they were forced to say to themselves: 'I wish I had told my father and mother how grateful I was for all that they did for me.' It is only courteous and polite to say thanks when people are kind to us. It is just the same with God. It is an ugly thing to take everything as a matter of course and never to say a word of thanks.

There is the prayer which we call *petition*. Petition means asking God for the things which we know we need, not only the material things, but the qualities of mind and heart and character which will enable us to live well and to make something out of life. But, if God knows what we need even better than we do, and if God knows what is good for us better than we know ourselves, why ask him for anything? It often happens in life that an older and a wiser person knows very well that something would be good for a younger person; but he does not know whether the younger person would accept it, if he offered it, and sometimes he even knows that the younger person would refuse to accept it. Often God cannot give us the things we need until we are prepared to consent to take them; and petition means asking God to give us the things which he knows we need, and telling him that we are ready now to take them. In fact, the best kind of petition is to tell God what we want, and then to say to him: 'Lord, give me not what I want, but what you know I need. Your will be done.' Often a teacher knows that a boy would make a first-class scholar, but he cannot give him the extra teaching and the extra work and the extra study, unless the boy will accept them. Often a trainer knows that a boy would make a first-class athlete, but he cannot give him the extra training and discipline until the boy is willing to accept them. God knows what is best for us, but God cannot give it to us, until we tell him that we are ready to take it. That is why we must tell God that we are ready and willing to accept his gifts.

The last kind of prayer is the prayer which we call *intercession.* Intercession means praying for other people. It is very natural to pray for people when we love them and when we want the best for them. All men and women and boys and girls are children of God. If you want really to please a parent, and really to make a parent happy, then the surest way to do it is to do something for the parent's son or daughter. And it pleases God most of all when he knows that we love and care for others who are his children. That is why it brings special pleasure to God when we pray for others.

When we come to think of it, we can see quite clearly that, although God does know it all already, there is every reason for telling him about it in our prayers.

iv. There is another thing which we must remember about prayer, and it is one of the most important things of all. We must never look on prayer as the easy way out, as the way to get things done without any effort and trouble and labour on our part. God will never do for us what we can do for ourselves, and, when we pray, we must immediately do all we can to make our own prayers come true. It would be no good at all to pray to God to make us good at our lessons and successful in our examinations, unless we work and study as hard as we can. It would be quite useless to pray to God to make us good at athletics, unless we train as strenuously as we can. If

12

we are ill, it would be no good to pray to God to make us well again, unless we obey the doctor, observe the diet that is set down for us, and take the medicine which is prescribed for us. It would, for instance, be quite useless for a person with a stomach ulcer to pray to God for health, and then to continue living on a diet of fried food. Prayer is not God doing things for us; prayer is God helping us to do things for ourselves.

Someone has said that God has four answers to prayer. Sometimes he says, Yes. Sometimes he says, No. Some times he says, Wait. Most of all he says, If. He says: 'I will help you, *if* you will do everything you can to help yourself.'

It is the same when we pray for other people. It is no good asking God to help the poor people, or to cheer the lonely people, unless we are prepared to give something to help those who are poor, and to visit those who are lonely.

Prayer is not an excuse for being lazy and for pushing all the work off on to God; prayer is a way to finding the strength and ability to do things along with God that we could never have done by ourselves.

v. There is another way of putting this. Prayer is not usually escape from things; prayer is the way to find strength to bear and to overcome things. Prayer will not cure a condition, for instance, which requires an operation to make us well again; but prayer will make us able to be cheerful and calm so that we will get well all the sooner. Suppose we plan to do something on a certain day, and suppose we want the sun to shine, it is no good praying that it will not rain. Whether it rains or not depends on the natural laws on which this world is founded. What we can and ought to do is to pray that, hail, rain or shine, we will be able to enjoy ourselves. It is no good praying that we should win a race or a game;

what we can do is to pray that, win or lose, we should play fair, and that we should take victory or defeat in the right spirit. Prayer does not usually stop things happening; it enables us to bear them and to conquer them when they do happen. Prayer is not a way of running away from things; it is a way of meeting them and beating them.

vi. There is one more thing left to say. Up to this point we have been thinking of prayer as if it were always we who were talking to God; but prayer is not only talking to God; prayer is just as much listening to God. Prayer is not only us telling God what we want; it is God telling us what he wants. It is not only us saying to God: 'Lord, I want you to do this for me'; it is us saying to God: 'Lord, what do you want me to do?' That must mean that in all our prayers there must be a time when we stop speaking and when we listen in silence for what God wants to say to us. In prayer we must never be so busy talking that we never listen, and we must never speak so much that we give God no chance to speak. Remember in prayer always to have a silence when we listen to God.

There are very many people who only pray when they are in trouble and when things go wrong. But it is a poor kind of person who only goes to visit a friend when he wants something out of him. We ought to pray every day in life, for we need God all the time. We ought to pray before we go out in the morning. Maybe we will not have much time in the morning but we can at least pray the prayer that old Sir Jacob Astley prayed before the Battle of Edgehill: 'O Lord, thou knowest how busy I must be this day; if I forget thee, do not thou forget me.' And we ought always to pray before we go to sleep at night. It will make a difference if we begin and continue and end every day with God.

This book is meant to help you to pray. There is in it a morning and evening prayer for each week for a year. Sometimes people do not pray because they do not really know what to say and how to put it. This book is meant to help you every morning and every evening to have a minute or two with God. But I hope that this book will be only a start for you, and that very soon the day will come when you will not need this book to help you to pray any more, but when you can talk to God, not in the words of this book, but in your own words, as easily as you talk to your best friend.

William Barclay

PRAYERS FOR YOUNG PEOPLE

MORNING

O God, my Father, thank you for last night's sleep and thank you for today.

Help me to waste none of today's hours and to miss none of today's opportunities.

Help me all through today always to obey my conscience and always to do what I know is right, so that I may do nothing for which I would be sorry and ashamed at the end of the day.

Help me so to live today that at the end of the day I may be tired but happy, with nothing to regret.

This I ask for Jesus' sake. Amen.

EVENING

Forgive me, O God, for anyone whom I have hurt, or failed, or disappointed today, and for any wrong thing I have said or done today.

Thank you for all the new things I have learned today and for all the things I have enjoyed today.

Give me a good night's sleep tonight, and grant that tomorrow morning I may waken refreshed for work and for play.

This I ask for Jesus' sake. Amen

MORNING

Make me all through today, O God,
    Obedient to my parents;
    Respectful to my teachers;
    Diligent in my work;
    Fair in my games;
    Clean in my pleasure;
    Kind to those whom I can help;
    True to my friends;
    And loyal to you.
This I ask for Jesus' sake. Amen.

EVENING

O God, bless those who are not so fortunate as I am.

Bless those whose homes are unhappy and whose parents are unkind.

Bless those who are ill. Specially bless those who are away from home in hospitals and in infirmaries and who are feeling everything very strange and who are a little afraid.

Bless those who are poor and hungry and cold.

Grant that in my happiness I may not forget the needs of others.

This I ask for Jesus' sake. Amen.

MORNING

O God, thank you for making me as I am.
Thank you for health and strength;

> For eyes to see;
> For ears to hear;
> For hands to work;
> For feet to walk and run;
> For a mind to think;
> For a memory to remember;
> For a heart to love.

Thank you for

> Parents who are kind to me;
> Friends who are true to me;
> Teachers who are patient with me.

Thank you for this wonderful life. Help me to try to deserve all your gifts a little more.

This I ask for Jesus' sake. Amen.

EVENING

Thank you, O God, for everything that has happened today, and thank you for bringing me safely to the end of today.

Forgive me for anything I said or did today for which now I am ashamed.

Forgive me,

> If I have worried my parents;
> If I have disappointed my friends;
> If I have caused trouble to my teachers;
> If I have let myself down.

Tomorrow is another day. Please help me to do better in it.

This I ask for Jesus' sake. Amen.

MORNING

O God, help me to cure my faults.
Keep me from being
>   Cheeky in my conversation;
>   Sulky when I get a row which I deserve;
>   Lazy at my lessons;
>   Disobliging at home;
>   Too conceited when I do well;
>   Too discouraged when I fail.

Help me to walk looking to Jesus, and always to try to be more like him.
This I ask for his sake. Amen.

EVENING

Thank you, O God, for all the people with whom I have learned lessons, played games, and walked and talked today.

Thank you for all the people who have been kind to me today:
>   For those whose work and whose love give me the things I need, the food I eat, the clothes I wear, the comfort I enjoy;
>   For those who have taught me the things which I must know, if I am to do a man's job in the world when I grow up;
>   For those who are a fine example to me of how I ought to live;
>   For friends without whom life could never be the same.

Thank you most of all for Jesus, my Master, my Example, my Friend.
Help me to sleep well tonight and to live well tomorrow.
This I ask for Jesus' sake. Amen.

MORNING

O Lord Jesus, be with me all through today to help me
to live as I ought to live.

Be with me at my lessons,
so that I may never give up any task, no matter how
hard and difficult it is, until I have mastered it, and so
that I will not allow anything to beat me.

Be with me at my games,
so that, whether I win or lose, I may play fair, and so
that if I win I may not boast, and if I lose I may not
make excuses.

Be with me in my pleasure,
so that I may never find pleasure in anything that I
would afterwards regret, or in anything that I would
not like you or my parents to see me do.

Be with me in my home,
so that I may be kind and considerate, and that I may
try to make the work of others easier and not harder.

Be with me in the streets,
so that I may be a credit to my school and to my
uniform and to those who love me and to myself.

Help me to be the kind of boy you want me to be.

This I ask for your love's sake. Amen.

EVENING

Forgive me, O God,

> If today there has been on my lips any word that was bad or untrue;
>
> If today there has been in my mind any thought that was envious or jealous or impure;
>
> If today I have listened to things which I should have refused to listen to;
>
> If today at any time I have been ashamed to show that I belong to you.

Help me to remember that you are always with me, so that I will always speak the truth, and do the right, and be afraid of nothing.

This I ask for Jesus' sake. Amen.

MORNING

O God, all through today help me,
> Not to lose my temper even when people and things annoy me;
> Not to lose my patience even when things do not come out right the first time;
> Not to lose my hope when things are difficult and when learning is hard;
> Not to lose my goodness and my honour, even when I am tempted to take the wrong way.

Help me so to live today that I will have nothing to be sorry for when I go to bed again at night.

Hear this my prayer for Jesus' sake. Amen.

EVENING

O God, forgive me for anything that I have done today which I would not want my parents to know about and which I would not want you to see.

Forgive me for anything in today which I could have done very much better than I did it.

Forgive me for wasting my time, and for spending my time on the wrong things.

Forgive me for everything for which I am sorry now; and help me to sleep well tonight, and to do better tomorrow.

This I ask for Jesus' sake. Amen.

MORNING

Help me today, O God,

At school to concentrate on my work, and not to let
my thoughts wander;

At games to play hard and to play fair;

At home to do my share in the work without grumbling and without having to be asked twice;

In my leisure time to enjoy myself in such a way that
I will do good to myself and no harm to others.

Help me to make this a happy day for myself and for all
whom I meet.

This I ask for Jesus' sake. Amen.

EVENING

O God, bless those who have to work while I sleep:

Those who work on the night shift in the works and
factories and the shipyards and the mines;

Those who go on journeys on the roads and the
railways, by sea and in the air, to bring us our
letters, our newspapers, our food in the morning;

Police and watchmen who through the night protect
the public peace and safety;

Doctors and nurses and all who through the night
must care for those who are ill and in pain.

Help me to remember all those whose work keeps the
world and its affairs going, while I sleep.

I know that you never slumber or sleep, and that your
care for me and your watch over me are unsleeping and
unceasing. Help me to sleep without fear, and to
waken refreshed tomorrow.

This I ask for the sake of Jesus, my Lord. Amen.

MORNING

O God, all through today keep me
> From girning and sulking when I do not get my
> own way;
> From being envious and jealous of others who have
> what I have not got;
> From doing things with a grumble and a grudge
> when I am asked to help;
> From making a nuisance of myself by being obstinate
> and bad-tempered and disobliging.

All through today help me to make the best of everything
that happens, and to do with all my might whatever
my hand finds to do.

This I ask through Jesus Christ my Lord. Amen.

EVENING

O God, bless the people to whom I owe so much and
without whom my life could never be the same.

Bless my father and mother, and help me to try to show
them that I do love them and that I am grateful to
them.

Bless my brothers and sisters, and don't let there be any
fights and squabbles in this family.

Bless my friends, and keep me true to them and them
true to me.

Bless those who teach me, and help me to be a credit to
them.

Bless me. Forgive me for anything wrong I did or said
or thought today, and help me to do better tomorrow.

This I ask for Jesus' sake. Amen.

MORNING AT EXAMINATION TIME

O God, help me at my examination today to remember
the things which I have learned and studied.

Help me to remember well and to think clearly.

Help me not to be so nervous and excited that I will not
do myself justice, and keep me calm and clear-headed.

Help me to try my hardest and to do my best.

This I ask for your love's sake. Amen.

EVENING

O God, I know quite well that I bring most of my
troubles on myself.

> I leave things until the last minute, and then I have
> to do them in far too big a hurry to do them
> properly, and so I often come to school with
> lessons half-learned and work half-done.

> I don't spend all the time I ought to spend in work
> and in study, although I always mean to.

> I get angry and impatient far too easily, and the
> result is that I upset myself and everyone else.

> I do things without thinking first, and then I am
> sorry I did them.

> I hurt the people I love most of all, and then—too
> late—I am sorry for what I said or did.

It is not that I don't know what is right. I do know—
but the trouble is that I mean to do it and then don't
do it. I need your help to strengthen me and to change
me.

Please help me to do what I cannot do and to be what
I cannot be by myself.

This I ask for your love's sake. Amen.

MORNING

Today, O God, make me
> Brave enough to face the things of which I am afraid;
> Strong enough to overcome the temptations which try to make me do the wrong thing and not to do the right thing;
> Persevering enough to finish every task that is given me to do;
> Kind enough always to be ready to help others;
> Obedient enough to obey your voice whenever you speak to me through my conscience.

Help me
> To live in purity;
> To speak in truth;
> To act in love
>> All through today.

This I ask for Jesus' sake. Amen.

EVENING

O God, thank you for all the things and the people which
make such a difference to my life.

Thank you for

My parents and for all that they give me and all that
they do for me;

My home and for all the happiness and the comfort
which are always waiting there for me;

My friends in whose company I am happy;

My school and for everything I learn there to make
me able some day to earn my own living and to
live my own life;

Jesus to be my Master, my Example, and my best
and truest Friend.

Help me to try to deserve a little better all the wonderful
things which life and you have given to me.

This I ask for your love's sake. Amen.

MORNING

O God, help me to use today as you would wish me to use it.

Don't let me waste my time today. Help me always to know what I ought to be doing, and to do it.

Don't let me miss my opportunities today—opportunities to learn something new, opportunities to help someone in difficulty, opportunities to show those who love me that I love them, opportunities to make myself a little better and a little wiser than I am.

Don't let me quarrel with anyone today; no matter what happens, help me to keep my temper.

Don't let me let myself down today, and don't let me hurt or disappoint those who love me.

All through today don't let me forget Jesus, so that all through today I may try to make everything I do fit for him to see, and everything I say fit for him to hear.

All this I ask for your love's sake. Amen.

EVENING

O God, before I go to sleep, I want to thank you for
everything I have:

> For this bed in which I lie and this room with its
> comfort;
>
> For my home, for the food I eat, and the clothes I
> wear;
>
> For my books and my games and my hobbies and all
> my possessions;
>
> For my teachers and my father and my mother and
> my brothers and my sisters and my friends.

O God, I know that there is hardly one of these things
which I could get for myself. They are all given to me.

Help me to be grateful for them, and to try to deserve
them a little better.

This I ask for Jesus' sake. Amen.

MORNING

O God, you have given me life, and I know that you
    want me to make something worthwhile out of it.
Help me
    To keep my body fit;
    To keep my mind keen;
    To keep my thoughts pure;
    To keep my words clean and true.
This I ask for Jesus' sake. Amen.

EVENING

Forgive me, O God, for all the wrong things which I have
    done today.
Forgive me for
        Careless work;
        Inattentive study;
        Wasted time;
        Duties shirked.
O God, I really am sorry about all these things. Help
    me to show that I am sorry by doing better tomorrow,
    for Jesus' sake. Amen.

MORNING

O God, take control of me all through today.
Control my tongue,
   so that I may speak
     No angry word;
     No cruel word;
     No untrue word;
     No ugly word.
Control my thoughts,
   so that I may think
     No impure thoughts;
     No bitter, envious, or jealous thoughts;
     No selfish thoughts.
Control my actions,
   so that all through today
     My work may be my best;
     I may never be too busy to lend a hand to those who
       need it;
     I may do nothing of which afterwards I would be
       ashamed.
All this I ask for Jesus' sake. Amen.

EVENING

O God, before I sleep, I ask you to bless the people I love.
Bless and protect
    My father and my mother;
    My brothers and my sisters;
    My friends and my teachers.
Bless and help
    Those who are sad and lonely;
    Those who are ill and who cannot sleep for pain;
    Those who are poor and forgotten and friendless;
    Those who are far away from home;
    Those who are in danger anywhere by land or sea
      or in the air.
I know you love everyone and I ask you to bless every-
one and to bless me, for Jesus' sake. Amen.

MORNING

O God, all through today,
    make me brave enough
        To show that I belong to you;
        To refuse any dishonest or dishonourable thing;
        To refuse to listen to any ugly or impure word;
        To do the right thing, even if others laugh at me.
Help me all through today really and truly to try to live
    remembering Jesus all the time, and not caring what
    anyone says so long as I am true to him.
This I ask for his sake. Amen.

EVENING

O God, forgive me for all wrong things in today.
Forgive me for
    Disobedience to my parents;
    Failure to listen to my teachers;
    Disloyalty to my friends.
Forgive me for
    Being careless and inattentive in school;
    Being disobliging and selfish at home.
Forgive me for being
    A bad advertisement for my school and for my
        church;
    A bad example to others;
    A disappointment to you and to those who love me.
Help me to sleep well tonight and tomorrow give me
    strength to do better.
This I ask for Jesus' sake. Amen.

MORNING

Help me, O God, never to be envious, jealous, grumbling or discontented.

Help me never to take offence, if someone gets the prize which I thought I should have won, the place in the team which I thought should have been given to me, the honour which I thought I should have received.

Help me never to grudge anyone his success, and never to find pleasure in the sight of someone else's failure.

Help me to stop thinking of myself and of my own feelings as the most important things in the world, and help me always to think of others as much, and more than I think of myself.

Hear this my prayer for your love's sake. Amen.

EVENING

O God, help me to keep in purity my actions, my words, and my thoughts.

Help me to do nothing in secret which I would be ashamed to do openly, and keep me from doing things which I would have to hide and to conceal.

So do you control me that I may have every instinct and passion under complete control. Help me always to refuse to listen to anything which would soil my mind, and to reject every invitation to leave the way of honour.

Help me to speak nothing but the truth. Keep my words clean and let no foul or unclean or dirty word ever be in my mouth.

You have promised that the pure in heart will see you; grant me this purity, this privilege and this reward.

This I ask for Jesus' sake. Amen.

MORNING

Give me today, O God, the mind which can really learn.
Give me

> The attentive mind, that I may concentrate all
> the time on what I am hearing or doing;
>
> The retentive mind, that I may not hear and for-
> get, but that I may grasp a thing and remember
> it;
>
> The open mind, that no prejudice may blind me
> to truth I do not wish to see;
>
> The eager mind, that I may not be content to re-
> main as I am, but that every day I may try to add
> something new to my store of knowledge and of
> skill, and something finer to my store of goodness.

This I ask for Jesus' sake. Amen.

EVENING

Forgive me, O God, for all the wrong things that have
been in my life today.

Forgive me

For being careless and inattentive in learning;

For being thoughtlessly or deliberately cruel and
unkind to others;

For hurting the people who love me most of all.

For being disobedient to those whom I ought to
obey, and for being disrespectful to those whom
I ought to respect;

For disobeying my conscience, and for doing the
wrong thing when I knew the right thing.

Help me to show that I am really sorry by doing better
tomorrow and by not making the same mistakes again.

This I ask for Jesus' sake. Amen.

Fourth Month: Third Week

O God, give me all the simple, basic things which will make me able to be a useful person in this world.

Help me to be

> Honest, so that people will be able absolutely to depend on my word;
>
> Conscientious, so that nothing that I do may ever be less than my best;
>
> Punctual, so that I may not waste the time of others by keeping them waiting for me.
>
> Reliable, so that I may never let people down when I promise to do something;
>
> With a sense of responsibility, so that I may always think of how my action will affect not only myself but others also.

Help me to live in the constant memory that you see and hear all that I do and say.

Hear this my prayer for your love's sake. Amen.

EVENING

O God, before I sleep I would remember others.
I ask you to bless

The sick who will not sleep tonight;

The sad who are very lonely tonight;

Those in peril in the storms at sea;

Those who are travelling by land or in the air;

Those in prison and in disgrace;

Those who have no house and no home of their own;

Those on national service in the navy, the army, and the air force.

Bless all my friends and loved ones whose names I lay before you now . . . .
Hear this my prayer through Jesus Christ my Lord.
Amen.

MORNING

Help me, O God, to bear well the things which are hard
to bear.

Help me to bear

    Pain with cheerfulness and without complaint;

    Failure with the perseverance to go on trying until
I succeed;

    Disappointment without bitterness and without
resentment;

    Delays with the patience which has learned to
wait;

    Criticism without losing my temper;

    Defeat without making excuses.

Help me to bear the yoke in my youth, that I may make
something worthwhile out of life when I grow up.

This I ask for Jesus' sake. Amen.

EVENING

Thank you, O God, for all the gifts which have made today and every day so wonderful.

Thank you for books to read, wise books to make me wise, books full of information to make me informed; great stories to thrill the heart and to linger in the memory; poetry with all its beauty.

Thank you for music of every kind, for dramas and for plays and for films, for pictures and for sculpture and for every lovely thing.

Thank you for games to play; for clubs and for fellowships where I can meet and talk and argue and play with others.

Thank you for
My school in which to learn;
My home in which to love and to be loved;
My Church in which to worship.

Glory and thanks and praise be to you for all your kindness and your goodness to me.

Hear this my prayer for your love's sake. Amen.

MORNING

Help me to be a good son, and to bring joy and pride
to my parents,

> To work hard, so that I will not disappoint those
> who have high hopes for me;
>
> To show that I am grateful for all that my parents
> have done for me, and sometimes to tell them so;
>
> To be obedient to them, and always to give them
> the loving respect I ought to give;
>
> Never to use my home simply for my own con-
> venience, but to be a real partner in it, and to try
> to put into it more than I take out.

Help me always to honour my father and mother as
your law commands.

This I ask for Jesus' sake. Amen.

EVENING

Help me, O God, to be a good and a true friend,

> To be always loyal, and never to let my friends
> down;
>
> Never to talk about them behind their backs in a
> way in which I would not do before their faces;
>
> Never to betray a confidence or talk about the things
> about which I ought to be silent;
>
> Always to be ready to share everything I have;
>
> To be as true to my friends as I would wish them
> to be to me.

This I ask for the sake of him who is the greatest and the
truest of all friends, for Jesus' sake. Amen.

MORNING

Help me, O God, to be a good scholar and pupil of my
school,

    To study with concentration;

    To do my work with diligence and care;

    To be obedient and respectful to my teachers;

    To take my full part in the life and the activities of
       my school;

    To take full advantage of all the opportunities given
       to me to learn; and to make myself a good
       craftsman and a good citizen of my country when
       I leave school and go out to work;

This I ask for the sake of him who was the greatest of all
teachers, for Jesus' sake. Amen.

EVENING

Help me, O God, to be a good sportsman and a good
member of my team,

    To accept discipline and to train strictly;

    To play hard but to play fair;

    To play the game for the good of the team and not
       for my own honour and glory.

    To obey instructions without arguing;

    Not to resent it if I am dropped from the team
       because someone else is preferred;

    To be a credit to my colours wherever I play and
       wherever I go.

This I ask for Jesus' sake. Amen.

MORNING

O Lord Jesus, help me to be a good follower of you,
Always to follow your example;
Always to ask what you want me to do before I decide to do anything;
Always to ask for your help and your guidance;
Always to remember that you are always with me to hear what I say, to see what I do, to keep me from doing wrong, and to give me the help I need to do the right:
Never to be afraid to show my loyalty to you, and never to be ashamed to show that I belong to you;
Never to forget all that you have done for me, and so to try to love you as you first loved me.
This I ask for your love's sake. Amen.

Fifth Month: Third Week

EVENING

O God, forgive me for all the things that I have left
undone today; and forgive me for the things I have
left half-finished and for the things which I never even
started.

Forgive me for not saying ' Thank you ' to the people
who have helped me, and for not saying that I am
sorry to the people whom I wronged and hurt.

Forgive me if I have hurt anyone, or disappointed anyone, or if I have caused anyone trouble, or if I have
been a bad example to anyone.

Give me your help tomorrow, so that I may leave nothing
undone of the things I ought to do, and so that I may
do none of the things I ought not to do.

This I ask for your love's sake. Amen.

MORNING

Help me, O God, always to take the long view of things.

Keep me from ever doing on the impulse of the moment things for which I would be very sorry afterwards.

Help me to remember that, even if at the moment I would rather play and amuse myself than work or study, I must accept the discipline of work, if I am to make anything worthwhile out of life.

Especially keep me from any habits or indulgences or pleasures which would injure others and hurt myself, and which some day I would bitterly regret.

Help me to look beyond this moment, and even to look beyond this world, and so help me to remember that this life is not the end, and help me always to live in such a way that, when this life does end, I may hear you say, ' Well done! '

Hear this my prayer through Jesus Christ my Lord. Amen.

EVENING

O God, tonight I want to pray to you for people who
have to suffer and to sacrifice for their Christian faith.
I ask you to bless

> Missionaries who go out to other lands to tell the
> story of Jesus to those who have never heard it,
> and who have to endure discomforts, face dangers,
> and accept long months and years of separation
> from those whom they love;

> People who live in countries in which Christians are
> hated and hunted and persecuted for their faith,
> and specially Christians who live in countries in
> which they are persecuted and cruelly treated by
> others who also call themselves Christians but
> who belong to a different Church;

> People who live or work in circumstances in which
> they are laughed at and even despised for trying
> to live a Christian life.

This I ask for your love's sake. Amen.

' The fruit of the Spirit is love, joy, peace, patience, kindness, goodness, faithfulness, gentleness and self-control.' That is what Paul wrote to his friends in the Churches of Galatia (Galatians 5: 22, 23). Let us all through this month ask God to give us these lovely things in our lives.

O God, give me in my life the fruit of love.

Help me to love you so much that I will never forget all that you have given me and all that you have done for me. Help me always to remember that you gave me life and everything that makes life worth living, and that you gave me Jesus to be my Friend, my Example, my Master, and my Saviour. Help me to love my fellow-men so much that I will no longer be selfish and self-centred, but that I will find the way to happiness in doing things for others. This I ask for your love's sake. Amen.

O God, give me in my life the fruit of joy.

Help me always to be happy and cheerful. Help me still to smile even when things go wrong. Help me always to look on the bright side of things, and always to remember that, even when things are at their worst, there is still something to be thankful for. Don't let me grumble and complain; don't let me be a pessimist and a wet blanket.

And help me to find my happiness, not in doing what I want, but in doing what you want, and not in thinking of myself, but in thinking of others, through Jesus Christ my Lord. Amen.

O God, give me in my life the fruit of peace.

Help me to take things calmly. Help me not to get into a panic when things go wrong. Help me not to worry but to take things as they come, a day at a time. Help me not to be nervous but to keep cool, when I have something difficult or important to do. Help me never to lose my temper, no matter how annoying things or people may be.

Keep me calm and steady, so that I will never collapse, and so that others may be able to rely on me when they are up against it. This I ask for Jesus' sake. Amen.

O God, give me in my life the fruit of patience.

Help me to have patience at my work and study, so that I will never give in but always persevere.

Help me to have patience with people, so that I may never lose my temper and never grow cross or irritable, or blaze into angry words. Help me to have patience when things are slow to come and slow to happen.

Help me to have patience not to give up, when something takes a long time to do, and when it does not come out right the first or the second time.

Help me to remember that everything worth doing is hard to do; that everything worth getting is hard to get; that everything worth being is hard to be, but that the struggle and the effort are worthwhile in the end.

This I ask for Jesus' sake. Amen.

O God, give me in my life the fruit of kindness.

Make me quick to see what I can do for others, and make me eager and willing to do it. Make me always obliging and always willing to lend a hand. Help me never to be mean, but always to be ready to share everything I have, even if I have not got very much.

Help me never to speak unkind words and never to do cruel deeds. Help me to think the best of others, and always to be more willing to forgive than to condemn.

Help me to be as kind to others as I would wish them to be to me.

Hear this my prayer for your love's sake. Amen.

O God, give me in my life the fruit of goodness.

Help me to be in everything I do and say a good example to others, and help me never to do anything which would make it easier for someone else to go wrong.

Keep my words honest and pure. Keep my actions fit for you to see, and help me never to do anything that I would wish to keep secret, and that I would be afraid that other people would find out about. Keep all my thoughts clean, so that even the most secret of them would bear the full light of day.

And in everything keep me from pride and from self-conceit; and help me to think, not of what I know, but of what I don't know, not of what I have done, but of what I have still to do; not of what I am, but of what I ought to be.

Hear this my prayer for Jesus' sake. Amen.

O God, give me in my life the fruit of faithfulness.

Keep me always true to myself, true to my friends, true to those who love me and true to you.

Grant that nothing may ever make me tell a lie. If I give my promise, grant that nothing may ever make me break it. If I say that I will do something, grant that others may be able to rely absolutely on me to do it. Help me always to stand by my friends and never to let them down, and help me never to grieve or to disappoint those who love me and those whom I love.

Make me so straight, so honourable and so true that everyone will be able to trust me in small things and in great alike. This I ask through Jesus Christ my Lord. Amen.

O God, give me in my life the fruit of gentleness.

Help me never to speak an angry or a cruel word, and never to do a hurting or a wounding deed.

Grant that I may never find any pleasure in anything which would hurt any person or any animal. Help me to be as careful of the feelings of others as I would wish them to be of mine.

Help me not to be too rough and boisterous in my behaviour with those who are not so strong as I am. And make me specially gentle and thoughtful to those who are sick and sad and old and weak and easily hurt.

This I ask for your love's sake. Amen.

O God, give me in my life the fruit of self-control.

Please take control of me so that I will be able to control myself.

Help me always to control my temper and my tongue. Help me always to control my feelings and my impulses.

Grant that I may never be swept away in some moment of passion into doing something which would hurt anyone else and which all my life I would regret.

Help me to control even my thoughts, so that no bitter thought, no unforgiving thought, no jealous thought, no ugly or unclean thought may ever get into my mind.

Make me master of myself for I know that, unless I can master myself I can never make anything worthwhile out of life.

Hear this my prayer for your love's sake. Amen.

MORNING

Lord Jesus, help me to remember that you are always
with me.

Help me to do nothing which would grieve you to see,
and nothing which I would be ashamed to think that
you should see me doing.

When I am tempted, help me always to ask you for
strength to do the right thing and to resist the wrong
thing.

When I don't know what to do, help me to turn to you
and ask you for your advice.

When I am frightened and lonely, help me to feel that
you are there, and to know that with you I don't ever
need to be afraid.

Help me to go through life with you as my Friend and
my Companion all the time.

This I ask for your love's sake. Amen.

EVENING

O God, forgive me for all the things in me which have
 kept today from being what it might have been.
Forgive me for being
  Inattentive at school;
  Disobliging at home;
  Bad-tempered with my friends;
  Selfish and thoughtless in my conduct.
Help me tomorrow
  To concentrate on learning;
  To honour my father and my mother;
  To be generous and unselfish in everything;
  To be a good comrade to all my friends.
So help me to please you, and not to disappoint those
 who love me.
This I ask for Jesus' sake. Amen.

MORNING

Help me today, O God,

> To keep my temper and to control my tongue;
>
> To keep my thoughts from wandering and my mind from straying;
>
> To quarrel with no one and to be friends with everyone.

So bring me to the end of today with nothing to be sorry for, and with nothing left undone; through Jesus Christ my Lord. Amen.

EVENING

O God, thank you for taking care of me all through today.

Thank you for making me able to go out in the morning in good health, and thank you for giving me my home and my father and mother to come back to.

Thank you

> For all that I have learned today;
>
> For all the games that I have played today;
>
> For all the friends that I have met today.

And thank you for Jesus my Master and my Friend.

Help me to sleep soundly tonight, and to waken fit for work and play tomorrow; through Jesus Christ my Lord. Amen.

MORNING

Whatever happens today, help me to keep cheerful.
Help me
Not to grumble when things go wrong;
Not to be discouraged when things are difficult;
Not to get annoyed when I don't get my own way;
Not to sulk if I get a row for anything wrong that
I have done.
Help me, hail, rain, or shine, to keep smiling, so that I
may be what you want me to be—a light of the world.
This I ask for your love's sake. Amen.

EVENING

O God, I don't want to pray for myself tonight; I want
to pray for others.
I ask you to bless
Those who are ill, and whose pain is worse at night;
Those who are sad, and who are specially lonely
at night;
Those who are in strange towns and countries, and
who are missing their own homes and their own
people;
Those in danger at sea, or in the air, or on the land;
Doctors and nurses, awake and helping others, while
we sleep;
All the people I love, and all the people who love me.
And bless me and keep me safe all through the night
until the morning comes again; through Jesus Christ
my Lord. Amen.

MORNING

O God, help me never to allow any habit to get such a grip of me that I cannot break it.

Specially keep me from all habits which would injure my body or my mind.

Help me always to do my best with your help to keep my body fit and healthy, and my mind clean and pure.

Help me at present to discipline and to train myself, to learn and to study, so that some day I may be able to do something worthwhile for the world and for you; through Jesus Christ my Lord. Amen.

EVENING

O God, forgive me for all the wrong things that I have done today.

Forgive me

For blaming others for things which were entirely my own fault;

For being rude, and discourteous, and bad-tempered, especially at home;

For being rough, and unkind, and unjust.

Forgive me

For the things which I should have done and have not done;

For the times I lost my temper and my patience;

For the lessons I have left unprepared and the tasks I have left half-done or badly done;

For the things I promised to do and did not do.

The trouble is that I know what I ought to do, and I really mean to do it, but somehow it does not turn out that way.

Forgive me, and help me tomorrow

To do what I know I ought to do,

And to be what I know I ought to be.

This I ask for your love's sake. Amen.

MORNING

Even before Christianity came into the world men have
always believed that the four greatest virtues are
WISDOM, COURAGE, JUSTICE and SELF-CONTROL.
Let us ask God to help us to have them in our lives.

O God, help me to have in my life the virtues which all
men value and admire.

Give me wisdom always to know
> What I ought to do;
> What I ought to say;
> Where I ought to go.

Give me courage,
> To do the right thing when it is difficult;
> If need be, to be laughed at for my faith;
> Never to be ashamed to show my loyalty to you.

Give me justice,
> Always to be fair in thought and word and action;
> Always to think of the rights of others as much as
> of my own;
> Never to be content when anyone is being unjustly
> treated.

Give me self-control,
> Always to have my impulses, passions and emotions
> under perfect control;
> Never to be swept into doing things for which I
> would be sorry;
> Never to do anything which would hurt others,
> grieve those who love me, or bring shame to
> myself.

Hear this my prayer for your love's sake   Amen.

EVENING

Forgive me, O God,
>For the time I have wasted today;
>For the people I have hurt today;
>For the tasks I have shirked today.

Help me
>Not to be discouraged when things are difficult;
>Not to be content with second bests;
>To do better tomorrow than I have done today.

And help me always to remember that Jesus is with me
and that I am not trying all alone.

This I ask for Jesus' sake. Amen.

MORNING

O God, keep me from allowing any habit to get such a grip of me that I can't stop it.

Keep me from becoming so fond of any pleasure that I can't do without it.

Keep me from allowing myself to become lazy, and from getting into a state in which I don't really care whether things are well or badly done.

Keep me from allowing myself to do things which would make it easier for me to go wrong and which would be a bad example to others.

Help me to live in purity and in self-discipline, and in the memory that you are always with me to see what I do, and to help me to overcome wrong and to do the right; through Jesus Christ my Lord. Amen.

EVENING

Forgive me, O God, for all the opportunities that I have missed today: opportunities to learn more; to gain a little more knowledge or skill for my mind; to help people who need help; to say a word of praise or thanks or congratulation; to show those who love me that I love them.

Help me to remember that opportunities so often only come once, and help me from this time on to seize them when they come; through Jesus Christ my Lord. Amen.

MORNING

O God, your word tells me that, whatever my hand
finds to do, I must do it with my might.

Help me today to concentrate with my whole attention
on whatever I am doing, and keep my thoughts from
wandering and my mind from straying.

> When I am studying,
>> help me to study with my whole mind.
> When I am playing,
>> help me to play with my whole heart.

Help me to do one thing at a time, and to do it well.

This I ask for Jesus' sake. Amen.

EVENING

Thank you, O God, for everything that has happened
today:

> For the good things which have made me happy;
> For the not so good things which have taught me
> that I can't always be getting my own way;
> For successes to give me happy things to remember;
> For failures to keep me humble;
> For time at work, at school, at games,
>> with my friends and in my own home.

And thank you for this minute with you. Help me to go
to sleep thinking about you that I may rise tomorrow
to live obedient and true to you; through Jesus Christ
my Lord. Amen.

MORNING

O God, help me to be cheerful all through today,
Whatever I have to do, help me to do it with a smile.
O God, help me to be diligent all through today,
Whatever I have to do, help me to do my best.
O God, help me to be kind all through today,
Whatever I have to do, help me not to be too busy
to help someone else.
O God, help me to be brave all through today,
Whatever I have to do, help me to face it and not
to dodge it.
O God, help me to be reverent all through today,
Whatever I have to do, help me to remember that
you see me, and help me to make every word fit
for you to hear, and every bit of work fit to offer
to you.
This I ask for your love's sake. Amen.

EVENING

O God, bless all the people who are in trouble tonight,
those who cannot sleep because they are ill and
in pain, or because they are old and lonely, or
because they are worried and nervous and anxious.
Bless any who are in danger.
Bless those who must work at night,
doctors on call, nurses in hospital and infirmary
wards, policemen on the beat, those called out
to accidents, fires, shipwrecks.
Bless me now, and help me to sleep well tonight and to
waken tomorrow to live strong and true; through
Jesus Christ my Lord. Amen.

MORNING

O God, my Father, thank you for all the ordinary, every-
day things of life.
Thank you,
>For food and for a good appetite to enjoy it;
>For games and for physical fitness to play them;
>For lessons and for a mind to learn and to think, and
>for a memory to remember;
>For work and for strength and skill to do it.
Help me always
>To keep my body clean and fit;
>To keep my mind keen and alert;
>To give my heart to you, because you have loved
>me so much and have done so much for me.
This I ask for Jesus' sake. Amen.

EVENING

O God, before I go to sleep tonight I am looking back
across today.
Thank you,
>For any new thing I have learned today;
>For any good thing I have been able to do today;
>For any happiness I have brought today to those
>who love me and who want me to do well.
Forgive me
>For anything I have shirked today;
>For anything I have put off today;
>For anything which I have could have done better
>today;
>For anyone whom I have hurt or disappointed
>today.
Help me to sleep well tonight and to do better tomorrow.
This I ask for your love's sake. Amen.

MORNING

O God, my Father, give me all through today sound
sense to see what it is right to do, and strength of will
and purpose to do it. And, if I am not able to do it
the first time, give me perseverance to keep on trying.

O God, my Father, give me all through today an eye
which is quick to see what I can do for others, and
willingness to do it.

Help me not to do things with a grudge; and help me
to do what I am told to do at once, and not to need to
be told to do it again and again.

Help me today to bring happiness wherever I go, so that
I may find my own happiness in making others happy;
through Jesus Christ my Lord. Amen.

EVENING

O God, thank you for all the people who have been kind
to me today.

Thank you for the people who have patience with me
when I am irritating and annoying, and who don't
lose their temper with me when I lose mine with them.

Thank you for the people who have patience with me
when I am slow to learn and slow to take things in,
and who don't give me up as hopeless, when I seem
to make no progress at all.

Thank you for those who give me, not what I deserve,
but far more than I deserve.

Thank you for those who keep on loving me even when
I hurt and disappoint them.

Help me to try to bring joy to those who do so much for
me, by trying to be what they want me to be; through
Jesus Christ my Lord. Amen.

MORNING

O God, help me to think all through today in every word
and in every action and in every situation of what
Jesus would do.

Help me to think of how Jesus went to school and learned
and grew in wisdom, just as I must do.

Help me to think how he worked in the carpenter's shop
and learned a trade, just as I must do.

Help me to remember how he obeyed his parents, just
as I must do.

Help me to remember how he found people unjust and
unfair and unsympathetic and unkind, just as may
happen to me.

Help me to remember how his friends let him down,
just as may happen to me.

Help me to remember that he loved us all so much that
he gave for us everything he had, even his life, just
as I ought to do.

He has left us an example that we should follow in his
steps. Help me to follow in his steps all through today.
This I ask for your love's sake. Amen.

EVENING

O God, forgive me for all the things which have defeated
me today.
For the times
    When I knew that I ought to do something, and when
        I was too lazy to do it;
    When I knew that I ought to help someone, and
        when I was too lazy to be bothered;
    When I knew that I ought to keep quiet, and when
        I let my tongue run away with me;
    When I knew that I ought to keep my temper, and
        when I let it flare up and blaze out;
    When I knew I ought to speak, and when I remained
        silent because I was too much of a coward to
        speak.
O God, I always start in the morning meaning to do so
well, and I seem always to finish at night after doing
so badly. Forgive me; help me; and, whatever
happens, don't let me stop trying.
This I ask for Jesus' sake. Amen.

FOR SUNDAY MORNING

O God, help me to remember that this is your day, and
help me to use it differently from the other days.

Help me to use it to learn something more about Jesus
and to come to know him a little better.

Help me to use it to go to Church to sing and pray and
listen and worship with those who are the friends of
Jesus.

Help me to use it to do something for others—those who
are ill, those who are old, and those who are lonely.

Help me to use Sunday in such a way as to help me to
live better through all the other days of the week:
through Jesus Christ my Lord. Amen.

BEFORE GOING TO CHURCH

O God, in Church today help me to listen, to understand and to remember.

Help me to go to Church reverently, because the Church is your house and you are specially there.

When we all pray, grant that it may be just like speaking to you.

When I listen, help me to concentrate so that I will really hear and take in and remember what is said.

And then help me to go out and to put into practice all you tell me in your house.

This I ask for your love's sake. Amen.

MORNING

O God, my Father, help me today not to let anyone or anything stop me from being what I ought to be and doing what I ought to do.

> Even if people are nasty to me, help me to be courteous to them.
>
> Even if people are unkind to me, help me to be loving and kind to them.
>
> Even if people hurt me or insult me or injure me, help me to forgive them as Jesus forgave those who were crucifying him.
>
> Even if things and people make it very difficult for me to do what I know I ought to do, help me still at least to try to do it.

Lord Jesus, help me to live today in perfect loyalty and obedience to you.

This I ask for your love's sake. Amen.

EVENING

Forgive me, O God, for everything in which I have failed today.

Forgive me for

Losing my temper when I should have controlled it;

Allowing my tongue to run away with me when I should have kept quiet;

Allowing myself to have bitter feelings about someone else;

Refusing to listen to good advice and for resenting correction when I deserved it.

Forgive me for

Failing to do things as well as I could have done them,

Failing to finish the tasks I should have finished;

Failing to work my hardest at my lessons and my work, and to play my hardest at my games.

Forgive me for everything that I meant to do and failed to do, and for everything that I meant not to do and did.

This I ask for Jesus' sake. Amen.

MORNING

O God, help me to live well today.
Help me
    To do my work diligently;
    To face my temptations victoriously;
    To play my games whole-heartedly;
    To bear my disappointments cheerfully;
    To face my difficulties manfully;
    To give all the help I can to all the people I can
      willingly;
    To obey you faithfully;
    And to follow Jesus loyally.
All this I ask for Jesus' sake. Amen.

EVENING

O God, thank you for giving me another day of life.
Thank you for
> The things I have learned today;
> The games I have played today;
> The friends I have met today;

Thank you for
> The love and care I have received today in my home;
> The teaching and training I have received today in my school;
> The loyalty and friendship I have received today from my comrades.

Thank you most of all for Jesus,
> The Example whom I must copy;
> The Friend who never leaves me;
> The Saviour who forgives me and makes me able to live well.

Hear this my prayer, and give me always a grateful heart; through Jesus Christ my Lord. Amen.

MORNING

O God, I ask you to bless all the people who today will have to do very difficult things and face very great responsibilities:

> Statesmen who will have to make decisions on which the welfare of nations and even of the world depends;
>
> Doctors and surgeons in whose hands and whose skill are the lives of men and women and boys and girls;
>
> Those whose job makes them responsible for the safety and the lives of others;
>
> Those who are in positions in which by speaking or by writing or by their example they can influence the lives of thousands of people;
>
> Bless all such.

Bless me. You have given me this life and I am responsible to you for how I use it. Help me to use every moment of today's time and every ounce of today's strength wisely and well; through Jesus Christ my Lord. Amen.

EVENING

O God, help me to sleep well tonight.

And bless those for whom there will be no sleep to-night:

    Policemen on the beat;

    Workers on the night-shift;

    Sailors at sea, engine-drivers on the railways, motor-drivers on the roads, pilots in the air;

    All who through the night look after the essential public services on which our convenience and comfort depend;

    Doctors and surgeons and nurses, easing the pain or fighting for the life of those who are desperately ill;

    Mothers with children who cannot sleep.

O God, I know that you never slumber or sleep. Through the dark hours give me sleep and watch over me while I sleep, and be with those who work while others sleep.

This I ask for Jesus' sake. Amen.

MORNING

O God, give me all through today
> Grace willingly to say Yes, when I am asked to help someone else;
> Strength resolutely to say No, when I am tempted or persuaded to do anything that is wrong;
> Patience to say to myself Wait, when I am in too big a hurry;
> Resolution to say Now, when I am inclined to put off till some future time what should be done today;
> Obedience to say to you, Lord, What do you want me to do? in every choice which comes to me today.

Hear this my prayer through Jesus Christ my Lord. Amen.

EVENING

O God, thank you for today.

Thank you for

> Lessons and tasks which stretched my mind, and made it able to cope with still more difficult things;
>
> Training and games which left me tired, but fit for bigger efforts;
>
> Kindness which touched my heart and made me love people and be grateful to them more than ever;
>
> Anything in the world or in the things which happened today which made me think of you.

Thank you for the good things which I will never forget, and forgive me for the bad things which I would like to forget; through Jesus Christ my Lord. Amen.

MORNING

O God, my Father, help me to do the things which are
very difficult for anyone to do.
> To be obedient,
>> When I would like my own way;
> To persevere,
>> When I am tired and discouraged,
>> And when I would like to give up;
> To study,
>> When I would like to be out playing games;
> To help with the work of the house,
>> When I think that it is a nuisance,
>> And when I can't be bothered;
> To keep my temper,
>> When I would like to blaze out,
>> And tell people just what I think of them;
> To forgive,
>> When I am feeling hurt and sore and bitter;
>> Help me to do these things.

At all times help me to find my happiness in obeying
you.
This I ask for your love's sake. Amen.

EVENING

Forgive me, O God, for all the wrong things I have done today.

Forgive me

> For forgetting the things I ought to have remembered;
>
> For failing to do the things I promised to do;
>
> For being inattentive to the things to which I should have listened;
>
> For being careless with the work on which I should have concentrated;
>
> Forgive me, O God.

Forgive me

> For doing things which I knew would annoy people;
>
> For behaving in a way that I knew would hurt people;
>
> For doing things that I knew would disappoint people;
>
> Forgive me, O God.

O God, when I look back, I can see now how foolish and how wrong I have been. Forgive me, and help me not to do the same things again. This I ask for Jesus' sake. Amen.

MORNING

Help me, O God, not to waste my time and energy on
useless things.

Help me

Not to envy others their gifts,

But to make the best of the gifts I have;

Never to wish that I was someone else or somewhere
else,

But to do the best I can as I am, and where I am;

Never to be jealous of anyone else,

But to be glad when others do well,

Not to worry about things,

But to take them as they come;

Never to be lost in dreams and schemes and plans,

Without doing anything to make them come true.

Help me to use my strength and my time wisely, bravely
and unselfishly, so that I will make the best of life for
myself and for others; through Jesus Christ my Lord.
Amen.

EVENING

O God, forgive me
> For hurting my parents today;
> For causing trouble to my teachers today;
> For failing to help my friends today.

Forgive me
> For being discourteous in my conduct today;
> For being unkind in my words today;
> For being unjust in my thoughts today.

Forgive me
> For the things I put off;
> For the things I did in too big a hurry to do them well;
> For the things I have left half-done;
> For the things I should not have done at all.

Forgive me, and help me to do better tomorrow: for Jesus' sake. Amen.

MORNING

O God, my Father, thank you for the world in which
I live.
Thank you
For all the beautiful things in it;
For all the interesting things in it;
For all the useful things in it.
Thank you for the life which you have given me.
Thank you for
My body to act;
My mind to think;
My memory to remember;
My heart to love.
Thank you for giving me
So many things to enjoy;
So many things to learn;
So many things to do;
So many people to love.
Help me never to do anything which would make the
world uglier or people sadder. Help me always to
add something to the world's beauty and to the world's
joy: through Jesus Christ my Lord. Amen.

EVENING

O God, bless all the people who are in trouble tonight.
Bless

> Those who are sad because someone they loved has
> died today;
>
> Those who are anxious because someone they love
> is ill today;
>
> Those who are lonely because someone they love
> left home today.

Bless

> Those who are tired because they have too much to
> do;
>
> Those who are poor and badly paid, and who have
> to do without the things they really need;
>
> Those who are unhappy because someone has been
> unkind and cruel to them.

Help me never to be selfish and never to forget all about
the people who are not so fortunate as I am. Help me
always to remember the needs of others and to do what
I can to help; through Jesus Christ my Lord. Amen.

MORNING

Give me, O God, a sense of responsibility.
Give me
> A sense of responsibility to myself,
>> So that I may never waste the gifts which you
>> have given to me;
>
> A sense of responsibility to my parents,
>> So that I may do something to try to repay them
>> for all the love and the care they have given to me;
>
> A sense of responsibility to my teachers,
>> So that all their patient teaching of me may not
>> go for nothing;
>
> A sense of responsibility to my friends,
>> So that I may never disappoint them;
>
> A sense of responsibility to those who have gone
> before me,
>> So that I may never forget what my freedom and
>> liberty cost, and so that I may hand on still finer
>> the heritage and the tradition into which I have
>> entered;
>
> A sense of responsibility to the world,
>> So that I may put into life more than I take out;
>
> A sense of responsibility to Jesus,
>> So that I may always remember that he loved me
>> and gave himself for me.

Help me to remember what I have received, and to use
what I have, and so to make what I ought out of this
life of mine, which cost so much.

This I ask for Jesus' sake. Amen.

EVENING

Forgive me, O God, for all the times when I was a trouble and a nuisance to people today.

Forgive me

For times when I was stubborn and obstinate;

For times when I was careless and forgetful;

For times when I was disobliging and unhelpful;

For times when I was far slower to learn than I need have been;

For times when I was late and kept people waiting;

For times when I argued when I should have kept quiet;

For times when I got in the way, and hindered people and kept them back;

For times when I made things unpleasant when I did not get my own way.

Help me from now on always to make things easier and not more difficult for the people with whom I live and work, and to help people on the way instead of getting in their way.

This I ask for your love's sake. Amen.

MORNING

O God, give me a sense of responsibility.

Keep me

From doing things without thinking;

From leaving an untidy mess behind me wherever I go;

From being carelessly or deliberately destructive;

From not caring how much worry and anxiety I cause other people;

From not even beginning to realize all that I get, and all that is done for me, and all that it costs to give it to me;

From failing to grasp the opportunities which are offered to me;

From failing to realize the difference between the things which are important and the things which do not matter.

Help me

Always to use my time and my life wisely and well;

Always to be considerate of others;

Always to realize all that is done for me, and to show by my good and cheerful conduct that I am grateful for it.

Hear this my prayer for Jesus' sake. Amen.

EVENING

O God, I know that you like a good workman, and I
   don't think that I have been very good today.
I am remembering now
      Things I haven't done at all;
      Things I have left half-done and unfinished;
      Things I didn't do very well, not nearly as well as
         I could have done them;
      Things I did with a grudge;
      Things I put off, and things I refused to do.
Forgive me for all bad workmanship, and help me to do
   better tomorrow;   through Jesus Christ my Lord.
   Amen.

MORNING

Help me, O God, not to be impatient when older people
tell me what to do and what not to do, even though
they often tell me to do things I don't want to do,
and to stop doing things I do want to do.

Help me to remember that they know what life is like,
and that they know from experience the things which
are wise and the things which are bound to cause
trouble.

And help me to remember, when I think that they are
hard on me, that it is not because they don't like me
but because they do like me, and because they want
to save me from mistakes and to see me do well.

So help me always to be obedient and always to listen
to advice.

This I ask for Jesus' sake. Amen.

EVENING

Forgive me, O God, for everything that has gone wrong
today.

Forgive me

For being cheeky to my parents;

For being careless with my lessons;

For quarrelling with my friends;

For causing people extra work and extra trouble;

For grumbling and complaining about things which
I knew that I would have to do in the end anyway.

Help me tomorrow to make life more pleasant for myself
and for everyone I live with and everyone I meet;
through Jesus Christ my Lord. Amen.

MORNING

Give me, O God, a will that is strong and steady.
Help me
    Not to give up so easily,
        but to stick at things until I succeed in doing
        them;
    Not to be so easily annoyed,
        but to keep calm, and to take things as they come;
    Not to be so easily led,
        but to be able to stand alone, and, if necessary,
        to say No, and to keep on saying No;
    Not to lose interest so quickly,
        but to concentrate on everything I do,
        and to finish everything I begin.
Give me a will strong enough always to choose the right,
    and never to be persuaded to anything that is wrong;
    through Jesus Christ my Lord. Amen.

EVENING

Bless those who are ill, and who cannot sleep tonight
    because of their pain.
Bless those who are in hospitals, in infirmaries, and in
    nursing-homes; and bless the doctors and the nurses
    who are trying to help and to cure them.
Bless those who are sad and lonely.
Bless those who are in prison and all those who are in
    any kind of trouble or disgrace.
Bless those who are far away from home, amongst strange
    people in a strange place.
Bless all those whom I love and all those who love me.
Bless me and help me to sleep well tonight.
This I ask for Jesus' sake. Amen.

MORNING

O God, bless my school, the headmaster, the teachers, the scholars and everybody in it.

Help us all to work so hard and to play so well that everyone will respect and admire our school.

When I am in school, help me to be a good and attentive scholar, and, when I am out of school, help me always to behave in such a way that I will always be a credit to the badge and to the colours which I wear.

Help me to remember all the time that I am at school that I am preparing myself to be a good citizen of this country, and a good servant of yours; and to that end help me

To discipline my mind to be wise;

To train my body to be fit;

To equip my life to be useful.

Hear this my prayer for your love's sake. Amen.

EVENING

O God, thank you for keeping me safe all day today from
the time I got up in the morning until now it is time
to go to bed and to sleep.

Thank you,

> For giving me health and strength to work and to
> play;
>
> For giving me food to eat, clothes to wear, and a
> home to live in;
>
> For giving me parents to care for me, teachers to
> instruct me, friends to work and to play with me;
>
> For bringing me to this night, and for giving me
> sleep and a bed to sleep in;
>
> For giving me Jesus to be my Master and my Friend,
> and to be with me all through the day and all
> through the night.

And grant that the memory of his presence may keep
me from all wrong things by day and from all fear
by night.

This I ask for your love's sake. Amen.